A CELEBRATION OF MOTHERHOOD
poems, thoughts, and words of wisdom

Michelle Gillett

The mission of Storey Publishing is to serve our customers
by publishing practical information that encourages personal independence
in harmony with the environment.

Edited by Karen Levy
Cover design by Wendy Palitz
Cover illustration © Juliette Borda and Alexandra Eckhardt
Text design and production by Susan Bernier

Copyright © 2001 by Storey Publishing, LLC

The information in this book is true and complete to the best of our knowledge. All recommendations are made without guarantee on the part of the author or Storey Publishing. The author and publisher disclaim any liability in connection with the use of this information. For additional information, please contact Storey Publishing, 210 MASS MoCA Way, North Adams, MA 01247.

Storey books are available for special premium and promotional uses and for customized editions. For further information, please call 1-800-793-9396.

Printed in the United States by Lake Book
10 9 8 7 6 5 4 3 2

ISBN 1-58017-384-5

Introduction:
On Being a Mother

As I waited to board a plane in San Francisco, a man standing behind me said, "It sure is hard to say good-bye!" How true that is. My daughter and I had just hugged and waved one last time before I took my place in line.

Each time I visit one of my daughters, I get a little more adept at handling the good-byes. I remind myself how happy I am that they have their own lives; I congratulate myself for having raised them to be independent; I marvel at how close we have become as adults and how pleasurable our visits are. Even though it has only been a few years, they have moved far beyond the defiant, unpredictable adolescent behavior that used to drive me crazy. They are living the productive and creative lives I had hoped and imagined for them.

As I stood in line and watched my daughter watch me board the plane, I thought how she has always been an adventurer. When she was eighteen, she asked my permission to join her college's hang gliding club. Against all my maternal instincts I said okay. I let her do it partly because soon she would be old enough not to need my permission for anything. I said it because I knew she

God could not be everywhere,
therefore he made mothers.

— Jewish proverb

was ready to try her wings. How many of us have wanted and waited for our mothers' approval of our flights and dreams? It's up to mothers to help their children learn the flight patterns of life and to give them the okay for liftoff.

Now I had to concede to a total stranger that, in spite of the fact that I have encouraged my daughters' independence, parting from them is indeed difficult. He persisted, "I can tell you are really close to your daughter." Sometimes I try to cover up my deepest feelings about motherhood as well as my constant revisions of it. My throat closed up as I said, "Yes I am," and I blinked hard against tears. All my efforts at managing distance and separation suddenly dissolved just because a well-meaning stranger was trying to make me feel better. He knew what it meant to me to be a mother.

My children have given me an identity I cherish: Mother. It began when I read *The Velveteen Rabbit* to my firstborn as she nursed. Like the Rabbit, I have become a bit worn in places, but mothering has made me more real.

When I was immersed in the work of mothering, my world revolved around my children; any other work I did was secondary to their happiness and well-being. So I was surprised one day not long ago when I overheard my younger daughter say to a friend, "My mother taught me the importance of being selfish. She always took time for her own work."

I hadn't realized the difference in our versions of reality. My version would have her saying, "My mother taught me the importance of being selfless. She managed against all odds to find a few seconds of time for her own work after she had done everything possible to make us happy and comfortable." So much of the confusion that defines being a mother is that the reality we experience is perceived so differently by those whom we nurture.

Many mothers struggle to work at jobs in ways that do not shortchange their children. Unfortunately, there's no formula to make combining a career and raising a family uncomplicated, no special key to unlock the door to succeeding at both. Some of us get lucky. But most of us just keep going, trying not to reveal too much about the complexity of our emotions.

When I found myself crying and telling a stranger how much my children mean to me, I realized that those complications might diminish when our children leave home but the stronghold of our love for them does not.

*Nothing will make you
as happy or sad,
as proud or as tired
as motherhood.*

— Ella Parsons

Mothers
and
Babies

Motherhood is defined by waiting: waiting for the baby to arrive, to fall asleep, to say her first word, to take her first step, to sprout her first tooth. I waited what seemed like forever for my firstborn. Late in the afternoon when the day was winding down, I would go into the room my husband and I had made into a nursery, open the top dresser drawer, and take out the little knitted sweaters, the impossibly small terrycloth sleepers. I would look at each one, then refold it and place it back in the drawer. It seemed to me that baby would never be born.

Waiting for a firstborn's arrival places you in a state of anticipation that builds until it possesses you completely even though you are still you, singular. And while more than anything you want the baby to enter the world and be yours, you know nothing will be the same again. I remember those weeks of waiting as a twilight time, a wishful expectancy bridging before and after.

Then she arrived — nearly two weeks late — a real person with a cap of dark hair and a mouth like a cupid's bow. She had ten fingers and ten toes and a concave place at the nape of her neck that I loved to kiss. All that waiting culminated in a kind of devotion that I had never before experienced.

Sometimes when I sat in the wicker rocker and nursed my daughter, I would think about my relationship with my mother. I wanted to be a better mother than she was. In fact, I wanted to be the best mother in the world. My mother was a very good one. She took my sisters and me to interesting places and read to us. She cooked wonderful meals and made sure we got excellent educations. She gave us a clear sense of values and a love of art and beauty. She taught us the importance of manners and being kind to others. She provided the security we needed to grow into ourselves. But she was not perfect. She was overly protective, too critical when we asserted our independence, and withholding of approval if we thwarted her.

I wanted to be a lifeline my children would hold on to rather than a shore they would some day swim away from. In that first blush of motherhood, I mistakenly thought that it was possible to love a child without making mistakes or having conflicts.

It wasn't long before my daughter was outgrowing those cute little sweaters and onesies I had wished over.

In no time, it seemed, she was standing in her crib calling, "MAMAMAMAMAMAMA" in different octaves until she hit the one guaranteed to get me out of bed. Pretty soon, she had a little sister.

In the back of every mother's mind is the knowledge of how quickly time passes and how important it is to enjoy every moment of our children's infancy and childhood. But it's hard to derive pleasure from days when it seems like the baby will never stop crying, the toddler's tantrum will never be over, and every hamper in the house is overflowing with dirty diapers and burpy cloths.

There isn't a frazzled mother on the planet who hasn't at one time or another wished herself back to the future, where her own life can resume just where it left off before she became irrevocably connected to these small, demanding human beings.

But in spite of the occasional longing and regret, a powerful bond ties mothers to their children. What mother doesn't remember the strength of her newborn's grasp? The moment a new baby curls her tiny fingers around one of ours is like a secret handshake: It signifies the agreement we extend to our children when they become ours. The connection is permanent.

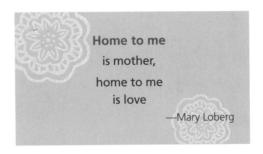

Home to me
is mother,
home to me
is love
—Mary Loberg

Who can forget the attitude of mothering?
Toss me a baby and without bothering
To blink, I'll catch her, sling him on a hip.

— Rita Dove, *Mother Love: Poems*

He lay in his cradle... his long cry threaded our world
to every other and the pull of every mother answering.
There were worlds without money, without sun, without
presidents, but there were no worlds without mothers.

— Naomi Shahib Nye, from *I've Always Meant
to Tell You: Letters to Our Mothers*

It would be years before I would comprehend "maternal instinct"— the effortless knowledge women allegedly acquired with birth — as a cultural invention that kept the hard work of motherhood invisible to anyone outside the field.

— Mary Kay Blakely, *American Mom: Motherhood, Politics, and Humble Pie*

I dream of giving birth
to a child who will ask
"Mother, what was war?"

— Eve Miriam

But love of an infant is of a different order. It is twinned love, all absorbing, a blur of boundaries and messages.

— Louise Erdich, *The Blue Jay's Dance: A Birth Year*

More times than I could count, in those early days, I was stopped in the grocery store by some kindly matron who exclaimed over my burbling pastel lump of baby: "Don't you wish you could keep them like that forever?" Exactly that many times, I bit the urge to shout back, "Are you out of your mind?"

— Barbara Kingsolver, *High Tide in Tucson*

A mother is not a person to lean on
but a person to make leaning unnecessary.

— Dorothy Canfield Fisher

Mothers
and
Young Children

For me, childhood was long hours of playing. On weekends, I played with my best friend Susie, who lived in the next town. Our parents would drop us off at one another's houses early Saturday morning and we would spend the day inventing dramas with our dolls or playing jacks or weaving pot holders on little plastic looms or pretending to be princesses or orphans or orphaned princesses.

After school, I played on the "island" at the end of our street with my friend Eddie. The island was a mound of spindly pines and maple trees, capped by a large boulder. The boulder was broad, slightly concave, and sloped like a giant's outstretched palm. Two children could sit on it comfortably and gaze across the street to an imagined distance where we survived shipwrecks and kidnappings by pirates and outlaws. We battled enemy soldiers and saved our neighborhood from the forces of evil.

The woods that bordered one end of our street offered still more opportunities. Sometimes I would go there by myself with my favorite doll and a book and sit on a mossy log and read. When Eddie and I went there together, we hunted frogs and salamanders, played hide and seek, or pretended to be soldiers. More often than not, Eddie's little brother George accompanied us. We viewed George as a nuisance and assigned him only minor roles — he was always the bad guy or the dutiful sidekick.

One spring afternoon, the three of us met after school and headed for the woods for a game of hide and seek. As we walked along the path, Eddie found a plank lying in the underbrush. "I have a great idea," he said. We each carried one end of the plank, George trailing behind us, to what we called "the swamp." At that time, I thought of the swamp as an enormous bog of bubbling quicksand that sucked down those foolish enough to walk too close to its edge. It was the place our mothers always warned us about. We certainly weren't allowed to play near it.

Eddie's great idea involved angling the plank across the swamp. He told us we would have a test. If we succeeded

My Mother
Who ran to help me when I fell
And would some pretty story tell,
Or kiss the place to make it well?
My mother.

— Ann Taylor

at walking across the swamp on the plank without falling in, we would be allowed to join the very special and exclusive club he had just created. He went first. As he watched his brother balance like a tightrope walker across the wobbly plank, George stepped too close to the edge of the swamp. All of a sudden he was sliding down the muddy bank, grabbing for twigs and roots and yelling for his mother. Eddie and I froze — he mid-plank, me on the other side of the bog.

At the time, I remember thinking that his mother could not possibly hear him. Their house was way down the street, and she was undoubtedly in the kitchen at the back of the house, starting supper and listening to the radio. Eddie and I watched, helpless, as George slid closer and closer to that devouring mouth of muck, all the while screaming, "Mommy! HELP!"

Suddenly, his mother came flying through the woods like a huge white dove. Just home from work, still wearing her white nurse's uniform, she raced down through the trees and grabbed George by the arms, just in time to lift him away from the sucking mud. I don't remember the trouble we were in, but I do remember feeling like I had witnessed a miracle.

When I had my own children, who found their own woods for acting out their imaginary adventures, I became aware of what childhood is like in those thickets — full of wonder and magic and carefree play, but often containing a "swamp" or some kind of danger where it's easy to slip and fall. It was only after I had children of my own that I understood how mothers are able to hear their babies across immeasurable distances.

This is my time:
the twilight closing in,
a hissing on the ring,
stove noises, kettle steam,
children's kisses.

— Eavan Boland

How can one explain all the time and thought that goes into raising a child, all the opportunities for mistakes, all the chances to recover and try again? How does one break the news that nothing permanent can be formed in an instant — children are not weaned, potty trained, taught manners, introduced to civilization in one or two tries — as everyone seems to imagine.

— Mary Kay Blakely, *American Mom:
Motherhood, Politics, and Humble Pie*

[N]ot only do moms get very mad, they also get very bored. This is a closely guarded secret, as if the myth of maternal bliss is so sacrosanct that we can't admit these feelings to ourselves. But you mention these feelings to other mothers, and they all say, "Yes, yes!"

— Anne Lamott, from *Mothers Who Think*

Some are kissing mothers
and some are scolding mothers,
but it is love just the same,
and most mothers
kiss and scold together.

— Pearl S. Buck

A mother understands what a child does not say.

— Jewish proverb

A mother is a person who, seeing there are only four pieces of pie, announces she never did care for pie.

— Tenneva Jordan

A rich child sits on a poor mother's lap.

— Spanish proverb

You read that the average five-year-old asks 437 questions a day and you feel proud that your child is above average.

— Liane Kupfersberg Carter

*Being a mother
enables one to influence
the future.*

— Jane Sellman

Mothers
and
Teenagers

I opened my eyes in the predawn darkness and looked blearily at the three-year-old standing next to the bed, pulling my pajama sleeve, yelling "Mommy, Mommy, wake up!"

"What is it, sweetie?" I asked, trying to mask my alarm at the urgency in her voice.

She brought her small face close to mine. "There is a witch under my bed!"

I bolted upright. "What?" I said. "And you left your sister alone with her?"

Granted, I was only partially awake, and the conscious part of me was not entirely rational at that hour. My daughter gave me a look that indicated she wondered where I'd earned my mothering credentials and toddled back to the room she shared with her little sister to contend with the witch herself or possibly forget the entire ordeal.

When my daughters became teenagers, I realized that the witch still haunted our house. I could sense her presence when the air bristled with arguments over who could wear whose sweater, who had borrowed whose jeans, who had gone through whose drawer in search of a tank top. I could feel the draft of her broom whisking by when bedroom doors slammed and one or the other of my offspring yelled, "I'm never speaking to you again!" I figured I'd know the witch was gone for good when I heard one of them say to the other, "My tank top? Of course you can borrow it. Wear it in good health. Perhaps you'd like to borrow my new shoes as well?"

I tried to vanquish evil vibes by being a good mediator, not playing favorites, listening to both sides of the story, upholding the value of compromise. But teenagers make it almost impossible for a mother to be fair. Learning to divide the last cupcake in exact halves is an easily learned skill when they are little; trying to provide equal rights to warring adolescents is an exercise in futility.

When rivalry flew through the air, casting dark spells over clothes and makeup, minutes in the bathroom or on the phone, and parental attention, all I could think about was how happy I'd be when the witch was banished once and for all from our domestic kingdom. But vanquishing the witch also meant that my children were finished with adolescence and packing their bags to leave home.

Before I knew it, my fantasy of an orderly house, manageable laundry piles, a telephone that didn't ring off the hook, and the ability to listen to music of my own choice became a reality. Gone for good were the sounds of the hair dryer humming, the telephone ringing, the stereo blaring, and those gangly boys hanging out in the kitchen, waiting for my daughters and their friends chattering upstairs to respond to their presence. When children close the door on adolescence, they leave their mothers on the other side. We watch them move toward their identities in the world and away from the witches under the bed.

As pleasant as it is to no longer pull wads of long hair from the drain, roll endless pairs of socks, and hear sound emanating everywhere, I actually miss the mood swings, the meltdowns, the attitudes that plague adolescents. I even feel a little nostalgic for the arguments over whose turn it is to do the dishes. But most of all, I miss the energy, spontaneity, and joy that are the blessings of teenagers.

Teenage boys: graceful, gauche, wafting musk through the room, vigorous, lit from the inside by a barely restrained power, an untouched and misunderstood virility — most of them so scared of their own shadows and what the world holds in store that they can't leave the house unless they're wearing clothes big enough to hide in.

— Sallie Tisdale, from *Mothers Who Think*

She's eighteen now, and when I look at her, I feel I don't know her. Some days I don't even like her, and I think if I could just tell this to someone it wouldn't seem so scary. No matter what I say, it's not what she wants to hear. No matter what she does, I'm alarmed, and it's all I can do to stop myself from imposing some "curfew" or "rule" or "punishment" I haven't the energy to enforce.

— Carol Lucci Wisner, from *In Short*

Over the years I have learned that motherhood is much like an austere religious order, the joining of which obligates one to relinquish all personal possessions.

— Nancy Stahl, *If It's Raining,*
This Must Be the Weekend

Making the decision to have a child — it's momentous. It is to decide forever to have your heart go walking around outside your body.

— Elizabeth Stone

Almost every adolescent will break almost every rule, at least once, before understanding why the rule is there.

— Mary Kay Blakely, *American Mom:*
Motherhood, Politics, and Humble Pie

Find the child,
going high and descending there — up and down,
up, down again —
her mittens bright as finger paints and holding
a crust of weather now: twelve years of age
in a thigh-length coat,
unable to explain a sense of ease in
those safe curves, that seasonless canter.

— Eavan Boland

The Community
of Mothers

My daughters' visits home are less frequent now that they are settled into their adult lives. But we've agreed that they'll always come home for Christmas. It wasn't all that long ago when the holidays were less a time of eager preparation and anticipation and more a series of crises set off by adolescent mood swings and miscommunication. The little girls who once tiptoed downstairs to open their stockings before the sun rose on Christmas morning became teenagers who would have slept until noon if they didn't have to go to their grandparents' house for Christmas dinner. Back then I would have cheerfully bought my offspring tickets to somewhere else for the holidays.

The best solution for avoiding lethal confrontation during their high school years was to spend less time in each other's company. My daughters therefore spent a lot of time at the homes of their best friends, Julie and Jenny.

According to my children, their friends' mothers always served dinner on time and the nourishment included large portions of praise and affection. Those mothers didn't worry and scold the way I did. Where I was rigid, they were not. Where I was uncertain, they were seasoned. When I reached the end of my rope, they held out a fresh, new piece.

My daughters and I survived those tumultuous years because of the haven their friends' mothers provided. When my children went to their best friends' houses, I knew they were safe. Another mother was listening and looking out for them.

Julie's mom was perfect in my younger daughter's eyes. She had raised eight children and seen just about everything. In fact, her buttons had been pushed so many times that she had reprogrammed herself years ago. She knew the right responses before the questions were asked. What she did best was treat my younger daughter like one of the tribe. She was always ready with a hug for the tears. And she could make my daughter realize — in a way that I couldn't — that the extravagantly expensive dress she wanted for the prom wouldn't guarantee her a good time no matter what the price tag read.

Jenny's mother was also very different from me. She kept house casually. A single mom, she and Jenny and my daughter would spend an evening painting their toenails and talking about dating. At our house, I painted walls and talked about curfews. My daughter and Jenny decided they were mature enough to travel through Europe during the summer after their sophomore year in high school. Maturity aside, I knew two sixteen-year-olds lacked experience about the world. A mother's worst fears and a daughter's burgeoning self-assurance can ignite the most volatile conflicts. My daughter didn't go to Europe that summer. She also didn't speak to me for days. I knew Jenny's mother supported the idea of the trip to Europe. She was a freer spirit, a greater advocate of letting teenagers be independent. But we respected each other's different modes of mothering, and she respected my decision.

Several years ago, a few days before she was due to arrive for the holidays, my younger daughter called to tell me that Julie's mother had died of cancer after being in remission for years. A few days later, my other daughter called with equally sad news. Jenny had phoned to say that her mother had died suddenly from a cerebral hemorrhage. The coincidence of these two mothers dying within days of each other the week before Christmas was almost too much to comprehend. I felt a deep sense of loss in my entire being.

My sympathy extended not just to my daughters' friends and their families but also to the community of motherhood. Both Jenny's and Julie's mothers played vital roles in my children's lives. I am not solely responsible for the independent, intelligent, thoughtful young women who arrive home each Christmas or for the closeness we now share. I have other mothers to thank.

The Mother's Day that means something, the Mother's Day that is not a duty but a real holiday, is about the perfect mother. It is about the mother before she becomes the human being, when she is still the center of our universe, when we are very young.

They are not long, the days of construction paper and gilded rigatoni. That's why we save those things so relentlessly, why the sisterhood of motherhood, those of us who can instantly make friends with a stranger by discussing colic and orthodonture, have as our coat of arms a sheet of small handprints executed in finger paint.

— Anna Quindlen, *Thinking Out Loud*

No song or poem will bear my mother's name. Yet so many of the stories that I write, that we all write, are my mother's stories.

— Alice Walker, *In Search of Our Mothers Gardens*

Some days I am made up of a thousand mothers who have given one ironic look, one laugh at the right moment, one exasperated wave, one acknowledgement. Mothering is a subtle art whose rhythm we collect and learn, as much from one another as by instinct.

— Louise Erdrich, *The Blue Jay's Dance: A Birth Year*

For finding your mother,
There's one certain test.
You must look for the creature
who loves you the best.

— David Kirk, *Little Miss Spider:*
A Christmas Wish

Blueprints

I search the sidewalk
cracks for evidence
of mothers' backs
carelessly broken.
Oh, baby, sing me the song
my mother sang me,
Help me keep my list
of hopes in hand.
Sit with me
a little longer, then
look at the map
I've unfolded below you
like a net.

—Ellen Wittlinger

*Motherhood is a lot like
having to navigate across a field
covered with old car tires.*

— Anne Lamott,
Operating Instructions

Mothers
and
Adult Children

"**W**atch out for the rocks," my daughter called over to me. I am not an experienced kayaker, but I am skilled and cautious enough to be an unlikely candidate for crashing into a distant outcropping.

"Don't worry," I called back, "I see them."

We were paddling along the coast of a small island in Maine where we vacation each summer. There was no breeze, and the ocean was as glassy as a millpond. We angled our kayaks toward a sandy finger that pointed toward the harbor.

"There are some really big rocks just below the surface here," my daughter warned. But when I looked down, all I saw was undulating seaweed and sun-dappled sand. I started to feel a little defensive — does my daughter really think that I have become so befuddled that I am likely to broadside a boulder? And when did she assume the role of harbinger of imminent disaster? That's my job. I'm the one whose vocabulary consists mostly of words of warning: *Watch out. Be careful. Don't.* Besides, isn't this the daughter who donned a wet suit to swim across San Francisco Bay? Who joined the hang gliding club in college? The one who began shaking her head and rolling her eyes at a very young age in response to my admonitions, which sounded remarkably like the ones she was uttering now.

Luckily for me, she was one of those children who didn't need to touch the knife blade or the stove to find out what "sharp" and "hot" meant. But that didn't mean she wasn't interested in a challenge or in challenging my desire to keep my children safe from harm. When she wanted to try water skiing the summer she was ten, I sat with my back to the bay so I didn't have to watch. I was good at inventing disaster scenes; I could see danger at every turn. But by imagining the worst, I was able to put more conviction into my arguments about why my children shouldn't do certain things even though all the other mothers let their children do them.

My daughter's new sense of protectiveness and caution was instinctive: She had become a mother herself. Six months ago she would never have cautioned me about the rocks or instructed me about how to climb out of a kayak. A vision of me hanging upside down in the water or lying battered and broken on a granite ledge would not have entered into her mind. Motherhood has changed her perceptions of her loved ones and of the world.

She is fierce in her determination to keep her baby safe. It amuses me sometimes to watch the person she has become. Motherhood changes us in unexpected and surprising ways. "I'll never be like that," we say of our own mothers or those whom we disdain as being over-protective. My daughter carries sanitary wipes in every pocket to clean the surfaces that her baby might touch. She checks the Internet for updates on the hidden dangers in baby food brands. The world is no longer about her; it is about the child she has brought into it. All the instincts that make us able to care for and protect a fragile, helpless being rise to the surface and carry us across waters that can shift from calm to turbulent in the blink of an eye.

When she became a mother, my daughter did not turn into me, just as I did not turn into my mother — but there are similarities. She is ultimately responsible for another human being. It didn't surprise me that she knew exactly what to do with an infant or that she has become a childcare "expert" now that she has a child of her own.

These days, I have more trust in the ebb and flow of things, while she is more anxious about the world into which she is launching her child. It is a more dangerous place than it was when she was growing up. There are rocks and cars and dogs and cats and germs and dirt to worry about, and other, more threatening dangers, such as boulders, lying just below the surface of the water.

On our voyage back home, the wind picked up and the ocean turned choppy and I had to paddle hard against the current. My daughter and I were side by side as we turned into the cove near our rented cottage. We share something new now — a mutual understanding of the depth and fierceness of love we feel for our children. We are on the same waves and the same wavelength, navigating them in similar ways.

Mother love is the fuel that enables a normal human being to do the impossible.

— Marion C. Garretty

In search of my mother's garden, I found my mother.

— Alice Walker, *In Search of Our Mothers Gardens*

[W]hen my grown children leave my home for their own, "Where in the world are you going?" I almost want to ask. But we are, all of us, in motion: both away from the past, and toward it.

— Genie Zeiger, *How I Find Her*

The way of a parent's love is a fool's progress, for sure. We lean and we lean on the cherished occupation of making ourselves obsolete. I applauded my child's first smile, and decoded her doubtful early noises to declare them "language." I touched the ground in awe of her first solo steps, as if she alone among the primates had devised bipedal locomotion. Each of these events in its turn — more than triumph and less than miracle — was a lightening, feather by feather, of the cargo of anxious hope that was delivered to me with my baby at the slip of our beginning.

— Barbara Kingsolver, *High Tide in Tucson*

A Mother

When you are a child, she walks before you
To set an example.
When you are a teenager, she walks behind you
To be there when you need her.
When you are an adult, she walks beside you
So that as two friends you can enjoy life together.

— Author Unknown

It was when I had my first child
that I understood
how much my mother loved me.

— Author Unknown

Mothers
Growing Older

My mother-in-law bought her best girlhood friend a big straw hat with daisies circling its crown for her 80th birthday. Her best friend has always loved big straw hats. My mother-in-law bought the hat not just for a woman entering her ninth decade but also for the girl who still lives in the woman. The girl and the woman are the same. The hat acknowledges both of them.

I enjoy the good fortune of having both my mother and my mother-in-law in my life as they grow older. They have supported my children from the time they were newborns. They sat on small wooden chairs on Grandparents' Day at elementary school, applauded at recitals and games, graced graduations and weddings with their presence. And I love hearing my daughters talk about their affection for their grandmothers, who never judged or criticized a grandchild even when one or another arrived for Thanksgiving with orange hair or a tongue stud or a tattoo — or all three.

As a grandmother, my mother is tolerant of behavior and fashion statements for which she would have disinherited her own children. I have heard her toss off a compliment or two for a micro-mini or a belly-button-revealing ensemble; I've listened in amazement as she has doled out sympathetic advice to a granddaughter living with her boyfriend-of-the-moment. While parents and their children struggle with boundaries and limits, discipline and communication, grandparents can simply sit back and bestow their gifts of acceptance and unconditional love.

I have had time to get over resentments I felt about my mother's demands and rules and about my mother-in-law's expectations and formality. As all of us have grown older, we have opened new doors to understanding. Years ago, I couldn't wait to leave my mother's house, her watchful eye, her intractable ways of doing things. Now I realize that our mothers, as they grow older, have a tremendous amount to teach us not just about life and aging, but about who we are. Out of the struggles and the complications of our past has emerged a love that is tolerant as well as nurturing. Just the way love is supposed to be.

The mothers in my life wear different hats now — those of friend, advisor, confidante. Our relationships have changed as well. Both my mother and mother-in-law are a little more dependent than they used to be. They need rides and reminders from time to time. As I balance between the old and the young in my life, informed and educated by both, my universe has expanded.

One recent sunny summer afternoon, four generations gathered for lunch in the backyard. My granddaughter observed the clan from a blanket on the lawn and pulled herself up on all fours to investigate the possibility of forward motion and the edibility of grass. Finches fluttered around the birdfeeders, flowers spilled over the leafy green of the perennial beds, and for an instant I felt all the summer afternoons of my childhood accumulate inside me. I wondered whether my mother and mother-in-law felt the spirits of their own mothers in the air that day as they posed for photographs with the newest member of our family. When I look at those pictures now, I can still see the girl in my mother and mother-in-law. She never disappears entirely, looking out from under the broad brim of her hat, showing us that life is circular, that endings become beginnings.

When I stopped seeing my mother with the eyes of child, I saw the woman who helped me give birth to myself.

— Nancy Friday

But she is my mother; there is this indisputable biological fact which blocks my attempts at objectivity. I love her, and the change in her changes me, too.

— Madeleine L'Engle,
The Summer of the Great-Grandmother

I cannot forget my mother. Though not as sturdy as others, she is my bridge. When I needed to get across, she steadied herself long enough for me to run across safely.

— Renita Weems

My mother is a woman who speaks with her life as much as with her tongue.

— Kesaya E. Noda

You never get over being a child, long as you have a mother to go to.

— Sarah Orne Jewett, *The Country of the Pointed Firs*

She knew how to make virtues out of necessities.

— Audre Lorde, *Zami: A New Spelling of My Name*

My mother refers always to my grandmother as Mother but the term seems neither formal nor distanced. The word is her comfort. I learned early that a woman who loses her mother aches. Much happens in life and miracles unfold, but that central absence of voice and image persists. It's as though a room of the spirit remains just as it was the day my grandmother died, the day her illness was over and mother had nursed her through it into the mouth of time. In that room possessions are undisturbed and August air smells of roses. The town stands still; the hour, closed like a bud, pulls softly shut. You only have one mother . . .

— Jayne Anne Phillips